Dear Friends & Family,
I ho
the pa,
Hope you are too.
Reta Oberg

Poetry 2
Ponder

Poetry 2
Ponder

poetry by d'vine, llc

WESTBOW
PRESS
A DIVISION OF THOMAS NELSON
& ZONDERVAN

Copyright © 2015 poetry by d'vine, llc.

All rights reserved. No part of this book may be used or reproduced by any means, graphic, electronic, or mechanical, including photocopying, recording, taping or by any information storage retrieval system without the written permission of the publisher except in the case of brief quotations embodied in critical articles and reviews.

WestBow Press books may be ordered through booksellers or by contacting:

WestBow Press
A Division of Thomas Nelson & Zondervan
1663 Liberty Drive
Bloomington, IN 47403
www.westbowpress.com
1 (866) 928-1240

Because of the dynamic nature of the Internet, any web addresses or links contained in this book may have changed since publication and may no longer be valid. The views expressed in this work are solely those of the author and do not necessarily reflect the views of the publisher, and the publisher hereby disclaims any responsibility for them.

THE CHARLES F. STANLEY LIFE PRINCIPLES BIBLE
Copyright - 2005 by Charles F. Stanley
Holy Bible, New King James Version,
Copyright - 1982 by Thomas Nelson, Inc.
Printed in the United States of America
2 3 4 5 6 7 8 9 -11 10 09 08 07

ISBN: 978-1-4908-8271-0 (sc)
ISBN: 978-1-4908-8273-4 (hc)
ISBN: 978-1-4908-8272-7 (e)

Library of Congress Control Number: 2015908879

Print information available on the last page.

WestBow Press rev. date: 8/11/2015

Author's Note

As we ponder through life from childhood to senior years, the journey offers a path of circumstances and choices. Our choices determine the impact of our lives. When our heavenly Father, God Almighty, King of Kings, Creator of the universe, blessed Savior, is invited into our lives—not as an afterthought but as a participant to be included in daily decisions small and large—that is when life begins to take on opportunities to become an intricate part of His plan.

Today may be the time when you have a decision to make to move forward by including Christ, the Creator of the universe; He allows you to choose. If your answer is life in Christ, may I suggest a total surrender with no holding back? Strap on your seat belt; no matter the circumstances, He walks with you. May your focus be front and center on Christ, and allow Him to create a desire in your heart to become all He intended.

I want to thank special friends and family who have offered advice, encouragement, and support for *Poetry 2 Ponder*. The Holy Spirit and God's Holy Scriptures were the resources to complete this book.

Contents

A'frayed 1
Armor All 3
As Stated 5
By Whose Measure? 6
Check Your Expiration Date 8
Christ Here and Now 10
Construction Zone 12
Cover Story 13
Forgiveness 15
Designer Genes 16
Eternity 500, Sponsored by God 17
Fatal Distraction 23
For The Faith, Will You Contend? 25
For. Air. Ver 26
God Made You Special 28
God May Not Have Called You to Be a Quarterback 29
God of Glory 31
God's Holy Commands 32
Good News 34
Have a Heart, Preferably a Transplant 36
He Shared a Precious Gift 38
Heavenly Father 39
Here I Am 41
His Greatest Desire 42
Homeland Security 44
HSD (Holy Spirit Driven) 45
I Don't Fit, Thank God 47
I Say Yes, Lord 49
I Stink 51

If Only	52
It Is What I Pray	54
Keep the Change	55
Let the Past Be Past	57
Me, Me, Me	58
Mediocre at Best	61
Now Is the Time	63
Oh, Brother	65
Peace, Be Still	67
Please, Be Seeded	68
Power Up	69
Pretender or Contender?	71
Really, Who Made the Rules Anyway?	73
Redeemer Rewards Card	77
Salt and Light	79
Stirred and Shaken, Not Forsaken	81
Test-a-Money	83
That's Life	85
The AudaCity	87
The Eleventh Hour	89
The End Result	91
The Grand Stand	93
The Mirror	95
The Ultimate Offer	97
The Voice	99
The Warehouse	101
Today	105
Until Death Do Us Part	107
Unwrapped	109
What Is Truth?	111

A'frayed

Lord, my tapestry may need a tighter weave.
Old behaviors surface and cause me to grieve.
My threads are hanging bare—
Loose ends with some to spare.

Strongholds and bondage—freedom is eradicated,
Decisions and choices with boundaries understated.
It seems to be about control or the lack thereof;
It seems to be about surrender and His faithful love.

Left on my own, my chances appeared slim.
I decided to take time out and sit with Him
To make a stand, map a plan, take a look.
He explained all the answers are in His book.

I asked myself how I became entangled in such a snare,
Always blaming circumstances appearing unfair,
Never taking a look at the part I played,
Disturbed to be accountable for decisions I made.

Invariably, it is easier to place blame.
It's been about me so long; it's my only game.
I tell myself it isn't true, and that's a lie—
The easy road, if only I could die.

Here I am, broken and shattered,
Emptied of frivolous concerns I thought mattered.
Getting over me, the stressful part—
It is difficult to imagine an opportunity for a new start.

In response to the love He is giving,
My desire: honorable living.
He completely changed this heart that was hardened.
I am no longer a'frayed; my sins He did pardon.

Armor All

I'm a new creation;
I've had a transformation.

I have the whole armor of God: equipped I am.
I wrestle principalities and wickedness in the name of the Lamb.

Truth has been girded to my waist
To prepare me for what I may face.

I put on the breastplate of righteousness;
I will give my best—nothing less.

For the gospel of peace, I have shod my feet
To stand against the wicked I will meet.

I have the shield of faith in preparation,
Quenching fiery darts headed in my direction.

The helmet of salvation I will adorn;
For this purpose I was born.

God's Word: I have the sword of the Spirit. I'm a believer.
His strength, His power, His might defeats the deceiver.

Always with prayer and supplication,
May I be bold in my application.

In the name of the Lord, I will be strong,
Standing for His Word against what is wrong.

The mystery of the gospel I'm privileged to share;
To speak His truth gives evil a scare.

I'm a new creation;
I've had a transformation.

I have received the call.
Suit me up with armor all.

As Stated

As stated, I give you my word.
There was a day when you were assured
The agreement made would indeed transpire,
Regardless if it met your personal desire.

How did we get so far off track?
What are the basics we seem to lack?
Why is a person of honor seldom mentioned
And truth and integrity create tension?

What appears to be acceptable today: out-of-control behavior.
Yet criticism occurs if you speak boldly of our Lord and Savior.
In this society, are we not upside down,
Where trust and faith are rare to be found?

Rebellious attitudes and willful disobedience—
A plan is offered for our offense.
It begins with humbleness and honest confession;
A pardon is offered for our transgression.

How many ways can we justify
Desensitizing truth and values to settle for a lie?
The truth, His Word, a blueprint for life lived best—
The cure for my soul's restlessness.

Truth is available, and I pray you are drawn
To inquire, to seek, before the opportunity is gone.
The Holy God has given you His Word; it is true.
As stated, an invitation has been extended to you.

By Whose Measure?

By whose measure are we good enough?
What are the requirements when times are tough?
Who will be the one to construct the scale?
Who will describe success or determine when we fail?

Will my value be considered by likes and dislikes on Facebook?
Will I be evaluated by the way I look?
Who or what will I allow to be my influence?
Someone whose sincerity is perhaps a pretense?

Despite my best efforts, energy, and attempts to be a friend,
The harsh judgments seem to pile up once and again.
Who knew life could be this difficult, or so it seems?
Stress and offenses cause bad dreams.

What if I redirect my focus to God, my Savior?
What if I could experience freedom from past behavior?
What if I limited my time on Facebook and
put my face in His Holy Book?
What if a commitment was what it took?

What if I asked Him to reveal His plan?
What if I began to understand?
What if I asked Him to forgive my sin?
What if I asked Him to be my best friend?

What if I were graded on the cross,
And I understood the gift of life and what it cost?
Could I become a reflection of His glory?
Would I choose to let this be my personal story?

By whose measure are we good enough?
Will you listen to those who speak smooth words filled with fluff?
Will you give significance to those who distort the line?
Live life abundantly. By His measure, you were
created an intricate, amazing design.

Check Your Expiration Date

America, we have all sung about how beautiful you are.
The last forty years, our disobedience
to God has left a serious scar.
How often He protected us, and because
of who He is, we prevailed.
To honor Him, as a nation with integrity, we have failed.

If we continue on the same path,
Prophecy states we will experience overwhelming wrath.
He is waiting for obedience to bless all the while.
History will repeat itself if we continue in denial.

Time is of the essence. Will you stand tall?
Reality has come. Will you respond to the call?
To honor God, to put Him first, was an
intricate part of our foundation.
It was a time of blessing, respect, and consideration.

Christian has become a label many choose.
As persecution transpires, this title, deceivers will be quick to lose.
Freedoms are disappearing every day;
God's people are being told they cannot pray.

Does your life exhibit God's fingerprints,
Or are you sitting on the fence?
He has sent His own to share His Word.
His salvation plan is plain and simple—nothing obscured.

He has a best-selling book.
Have you taken the time to look?
He has placed a void in your heart
To allow you to seek Him right from the start.

God has made the call to us and to our nation:
Will you be a first responder in this emergency situation?
His voice is resounding in the air.
A reservation is required to be in His protective care.

America the beautiful, will you forfeit your place?
To exclude God, to continue as is, ends in disgrace.
He has called you; don't wait until it is too late.
Only He can check your expiration date.

Christ Here and Now

If I were to explain how
To live in Christ, here and now,
I would begin with complete surrender.
May I suggest a heart that is tender?

I would pray at every opportunity,
Mostly for others, sometimes for me.
I would request forgiveness of sins,
Knowing it is how restoration begins.

I would pray for a heart of gratitude;
Humble would describe my attitude—
A willingness to hear His voice,
To include Him in every choice.

As He leaves nothing to chance,
I would put Him first in finance.
This is an area I will not trim.
I am unable to out give Him.

I would pray for His covering and protection too.
Only He knows what I'll battle through.
All the details, He orchestrates
To strengthen my character traits.

Taking time for Him, I find
Faith, love, and peace of mind.
Mercy and grace I would freely give.
They were extended to me that I might live.

His Word, I could discern
Wisdom and His concern
If I were to try to explain how,
To live in Christ here and now.

Today I will pursue His holy presence—
An intimate relationship so intense—
That I might reflect the glory of my King.
For Him and you, may I be a blessing.

Construction Zone

The road of life may be riddled with detours;
Possible reroutes and transitions occur.
Warning signs in place depicting twists and turns—
It may be time to reevaluate concerns.

Barricades, concrete dividers, and flaggers are in place.
Surveying the conditions, it is necessary to slow the pace.
Potholes, hazards, excessive projects in my estimation—
A shoulder provided for an emergency situation.

Guidelines and safety features exist in the road design,
Sometimes we drift and cross over the line.
In life there are many construction zones.
You may have your own orange barrels with matching cones.

Detours take us away from the main road,
Sometimes taxing us with what appears to be an overload.
It can be a struggle to survive the elements;
Heavy loads overwhelm us, and we feel tense.

Exercising caution and considering our speed,
We look for the pilot driver to take over the lead.
As we are led through, traffic is slowed,
Bringing us back to the main road.

The main road was created for guidance to our final destination
By an amazing designer who offers complete restoration.
A navigation system is provided, a remarkable revelation:
"Detour closed: use the main road," per voice activation.

Cover Story

Well-meaning words expressed to give advice,
Complicating matters by someone's cover of being nice.
This can be dangerous territory to tread,
Overwhelming when perhaps too much is said.

Sometimes we are prompted to share our wisdom
When the timing or circumstances are not right for some.
You may be unaware of all the facts.
Emotional stability may be pushed to the max.

Words can be heavyweights that push the scale.
They can have the persona of a hammer adding another nail.
There is a time and place for issues to be addressed—
Not an easy task; confrontation can put us to the test.

Offering up unwanted advice,
Without the approval of Christ,
Ask yourself, is this God's idea or mine?
Aligned in His accord, or are we out of line?

Involving the Lord in the situation at hand
May prompt our hearts and minds to better understand.
Let your conversation with Christ be the first connection.
If He encourages you to proceed, seek His timing and direction.

When we have our own agenda, muting God's Word,
Results include boundaries undefined and motives blurred.
When the Lord is the counsel you seek,
Ask permission to proceed if He intends you to speak.

Words we deem necessary to share
Should be based in love and care.
Before you proceed in offering advice or correction,
Check the mirror for Christ's reflection.

Forgiveness

Forgiveness, an exorbitant gift,
Undeserved, a bridge to gap a rift—
A covering of freedom to heal the soul.
Forgiveness: without it we pay a heavy toll.

Resentments burden us with pain and grief.
Forgiveness is powerful in generating relief.
Forgiveness is not forgetting the offense—
Rather, discerning behaviors that may not make sense.

Forgiveness doesn't right a wrong,
Releasing us, moving forward to be strong.
Injustice can be responsible for bitterness,
Building barriers that leave us in distress.

Forgiveness is an extension of grace,
It is necessary to keep healthy boundaries in place.
There are those who may choose to say no.
Seek prayer if perhaps you should let them go.

Blessed are those whose transgressions are forgiven.
When sin is covered, there is hope, optimism.
By faith, forgiveness is extended to those who are sanctified,
An inheritance through Christ, with whom we are crucified.

Covered by His blood, we have been called to forgive,
Being kind, tenderhearted, as we were designed to live.
Forgiveness is a gift to give and receive.
To understand this kind of love, you must believe.

Designer Genes

Ancestors and heritage seem to intrigue.
We like to consider ourselves in an exclusive league.
Designer genes, we like to claim,
Any evidence that brings us fame.

All this talk about our history—
I prefer the future where I am free.
My genealogy, there is no need to trace;
I have been adopted by the God of grace.

I have been woven together in His tapestry,
A process designed to set me free.
A message to me, He did send,
Character flaws that did offend.

A makeover was in store;
Putting Him first was at the core.
His Word became my daily guide.
By faith, I was justified.

The path is clear—no detour.
In Him, I am now secure.
Blessed assurance, a gift He grants,
Regardless of my circumstance.

Jesus, I give You glory;
You are the subject of our story.
You gave your life, it seems,
That I might inherit Your designer genes.

Eternity 500, Sponsored by God

In the beginning, God was a Nascar fan.
He knew each of you; He had a personal plan.
The track requires prequalification and an entry fee.
His plan includes Father, Son, and Holy Spirit—all three.

Ovals, paper clips, road courses, tracks of every calibration—
He knows about each one and their location.
The national anthem, the air show, and the invocation—
As each race begins, respect is shown throughout the nation.

For drivers, owners, teams, fans, and crew chiefs,
He knew there would be times of celebration, times of grief.
Each team aspires to get to the front;
He knows each driver and who is in the hunt.

Line up for position, starting with the pole;
He knows the spotters, owners, teams,
and drivers all have their role.
Drivers, start your engines, all considerations made;
He knows your circumstances and strategies to be played.

A few laps around the track to set the pace—
You would be wise to pray for your day and extend grace.
The flag is green; it's time to go
As qualified, from fast to slow.

Communication between driver and crew chief a must,
He knew frustration and strong opinions will cause some to cuss.
There may be times when you're bumped, or hit the wall.
He allows you to respond to adversity; you make the call.

What are the chances you will complete all the laps?
Or will your chassis hit the wall and be left for scraps?
Only He knows what will transpire.
He knows your condition and your greatest desire.

Whether it's a tandem dance or a bump draft,
The beginning of the race or right at half,
You may need a correction to change your line.
He knows your position and who will be fine.

Officials will track your miles per hour;
Timing lines and pit stops are monitored from the tower.
Leading laps and positions scored
For Toyota, Chevrolet, and Ford.

Staying on track is always the plan,
Away from the wall, doing the best you can.
If possible, avoid the safety barrier,
And then the big one; what could be scarier?

Take advantage of the cautions as a rule,
A pit stop for adjustments, tires, and fuel.
Wedge and tire pressures checked,
Calculations to make sure all is correct.

It's a win; the checkered flag flies in the sky,
A burnout for the driver, who is seldom shy.
Points accrued for the chase,
Of utmost importance, where you place.

A trip to Victory Lane ensues,
A celebration with driver and crews.
Fireworks, interviews, and photos entail—
Sprayed beverage without fail.

Now you may think this is the end of the race;
It's only the beginning to what you may face ...
Whether you're a driver or one of the fans,
Packed in the infield or seated in the stands.

Did you know your chassis and setup were an amazing design,
And you've had a sponsor since the beginning of time?
You may need a course correction.
A fire suit may not offer protection.

To start the race, you make a request.
Start with prayer; you will be blessed.
Ask Him to make your slate blank.
Ask Him to empty your fuel tank.

Surrender your life to His plans,
To the Holy One with nail-scarred hands.
Do you understand His offer, His saving grace?
He died for you and took your place.

Do you believe, really believe, He will do what He said?
Are you waiting for a caution or a flag that is red?
Seeking Him through circumstances makes you a contender.
You may require a transplant—a heart that is tender.

Unshakable faith never judges by how you feel.
It serves best when you let Him take the wheel.
There are many race seasons in life
That are sure to include disappointments and strife.

There are plenty of testimonies to find in His Word.
With obedience and availability, victory's assured.
Once and for all, find your groove.
Your future contract depends on your next move.

Everyone who enters has a chance to win.
Ask Him for forgiveness of your sin.
His desire is to equip as needed.
The winner's circle is where He wants you to be greeted.

At the end of your laps, you will be at His feet.
Are you looking forward to the day you will meet?
On judgment day there will be accountability.
Believers will have a prepaid entry fee.

Don't let hypocrites stand in your way.
Even they may understand someday.
You will know the real deal;
His holy presence you will feel.

You can start today; you'll know the end.
Let me introduce you to my best friend,
Jesus Christ, Lord of all.
He will make the final call.

Not on Twitter, e-mail, or a cell phone,
No need to wait for a dial tone.
The meeting will be one-on-one
With Jesus Christ—God's only Son.

Eternity 500, enter today.
He has paved the way.
His desire throughout the race:
To see you in Victory Lane—an extension of His grace.

Fatal Distraction

The enemy of our soul offers fatal distraction,
Being unaware creates a slow reaction.
How often our focus is scattered or futile—
An empty facade disguised in denial.

How often our hopes appear to be destroyed;
Our hearts experience a senseless void.
Foolish decisions, cluttered with sorrow,
You question the future, the totality of tomorrow.

We seemed to have labored abundantly in vain;
The reflection in the mirror resembles someone in pain.
As you grapple with unrealistic expectations,
Disappointments occur on a constant rotation.

We may ask ourselves, why is this happening to me?
There is a desperate attempt for an innocent plea.
Perhaps we need to reevaluate
Consequences of choices we tend to underestimate.

Life offers up a cafeteria of choices we face:
Reality comingled with the dreams we chase.
Arrogant pride and wicked intent
Plunder the soul with the messages sent.

How did we allow ourselves to get into such a state?
A self-exam is needed before it's too late.
There is reproach in our perversity;
Only a Holy God could extend grace to you and me.

When you are capable of looking beyond yourself,
Handling the debris you've stored on the shelf,
Truth is certain; it trumps a fatal distraction.
A dynamic relationship with God requires you to take action.

For The Faith, Will You Contend?

A great battle is shaping up;
Judgment is coming for those corrupt.
There are pretenders, you should be aware.
The danger is real; deception they share.

False teachers and deceivers
Will focus their attention on believers.
Consider discretion with whom you confide;
His Word creates a great divide.

The time is coming; you should prepare.
Conditions will appear extremely unfair.
Mockers will abound in their own lust,
With attempts to belittle your sovereign trust.

There are those who choose to deny.
They continue in sin; they believe a lie.
Take comfort with a holy God.
He's in control; He knows their fraud.

When it appears grim,
Keep your focus on Him.
Be encouraged; keep God in your sight.
He will be the one to set things right.

The message was written; the message was sent.
Time is of the essence for all to repent.
Are you the one who is willing to defend?
For the faith, will you contend?

For. Air. Ver

Many have predicted when the world will end.
The truth you'll find in His Word, my friend.
There are signs; believers should be aware.
Spend time in His Word, and seek Him in prayer.

No marks, no chips, no requirements for face recognition.
Of utmost importance: your heart condition.
God's Word is holy and true.
Will you be counted as one of the chosen few?

As you meditate on the revelation of Jesus Christ,
Consider a holy God and His sacrifice.
Do you have the insight? Do you have the vision?
Time is of the essence to terminate indecision.

In our time, there's an abundance of deceit and lies.
Are you set apart from those who compromise?
Peace treaties are fragile; situations are tense,
With motives ruled by dollars and cents.

Moral conditions resemble a plague out of control.
The offenses sear and scar our souls.
National disasters will become commonplace—
A sign of what's in store for the human race.

False teachers will explode with force.
Will you ensure the gospel of Christ is your power source?
Stay alert, take warnings seriously, and heed the signs.
Know His Word; be secure as the world declines.

Be prepared to be caught up in the air;
Believers only, He will meet you there.
It is His Word; it is how it ends.
Forever with Christ, eternity, now it begins.

God Made You Special

God made you special; yes, it's true,
And gave us this day to celebrate you.

May you be strengthened and encouraged today,
Touched by His spirit, as is His way.

Peace and joy, some of His gifts
To lighten the load, to give a lift.

And there are more: sweet mercy and grace,
His endless love, His tender embrace.

His purpose for you, His plans the best,
His desire to bless you, to give you rest.

His love is incredible—how do I explain?
Look in the mirror; the reflection is plain.

You were created with detailed design,
Spectacular precision, and all that is fine.

Intricately woven, a pattern of you,
Specific instructions—a relationship to pursue.

On this day, I offer a prayer.
His love for you, we can share.

Now I understand the ultimate story.
I look in your eyes; I see His glory.

God May Not Have Called You to Be a Quarterback

God may not have called you to be a quarterback.
Perhaps you'll be asked to pick up the slack.
Another option: a wide receiver.
Now that's a blessing for a true believer.

Passes spiraled in your direction,
Add the running game for perfection.
Your slot may be to hold the line.
Without penalty, execution divine.

God may request a running back,
Someone with dance moves who can track.
Now you may be a guard
Who is working hard.

Or, you're playing defense,
With adrenaline and emotions so intense.
Focus on the center, then the snap—
A little play action, looking for a gap.

A tight end may be your place.
Most likely someone will be in your face.
You may be called to be a safety or a back,
Or maybe the one credited for the sack.

There is always a kicker in life,
Sometimes a game winner, sometimes strife.
You could be a backup with talent not utilized.
Circumstances change and dreams are realized.

You should evaluate the condition of the field,
Tempers in whatever climate show character revealed.
There are life lines in the turf and chains to measure,
Yardage gains, and plays to treasure.

The point: always be prepared
To ensure the gospel of Christ is shared.
The goal posts are narrow; choices are made.
Are you on the team? Is your position well played?

God of Glory

To convey our thoughts, may we begin.
Father, Lord, Redeemer, our best friend,
Your holiness is an awesome story.
We sing Your praise, God of Glory.

As we ponder Your truth and seek direction,
Your holy Word offers a course correction.
God of glory, You set things right.
You are the way, the truth, and the light.

Your hand is upon us in a world gone wild.
Your interest in us so intense we feel like an only child.
How do You explain a love like this—
All encompassing, with nothing amiss?

From birth through life, the end, the grave,
It was predetermined; You chose us to save.
May we express gratitude beyond measure?
The condition of our hearts we offer as treasure.

For You, we want to serve,
Showing to You love that You deserve.
As we worship and take time for prayer,
Through all circumstances You are always there.

Spending time with You today—
Incredible love—You take my breath away.
Let us celebrate; let us all say,
God of Glory, Happy Father's Day.

God's Holy Commands

(Reference: the Holy Bible)

#1 I am the Lord God; you shall have no other gods before Me.
Honor, power, and authority, we should give Him top priority.

#2 You shall not make for yourself carved images; you shall
not bow down or serve them, any likeness of anything,
You have a covenant with your holy King,
and it will bring a blessing.

#3 You shall not take the name of the Lord in vain.
His name should be revered; from lack
of respect we should refrain.

#4 Remember the Sabbath day and keep it holy; six
days you shall labor and do all your work and the
seventh day is the Sabbath day of the Lord—
A time of rest, and time to worship Him in one accord.

#5 Honor your father and mother.
Obedience brings blessings like no other.

#6 You shall not murder.
Pray for balanced temperament, should the desire occur.

#7 You shall not commit adultery.
This destroys lives and saddens the Lord's heart, you see.

#8 You shall not steal.
Only the Devil would encourage this kind of deal.

#9 You shall not bear false witness.
The truth sets you free; don't make this a test.

#10 You shall not covet your neighbor or anything he owns,
Including his house, his car, or his cell phone.

Commands are not suggestions.
They are not to be questioned.

Rules given from the Lord above
Are rules given in supernatural love.

O Lord, you gave us only ten.
You have to be asking yourself, *Obedience ... when?*

Good News

You know His Word; you know His requests,
Yet you've hesitated to give Him your best.
The cares of this world cause you to stray.
Good intentions and priorities appear in disarray.

You recognize how you've been short-sighted.
Time has passed since you've caused Him to be delighted.
If today was your only opportunity,
What would you do differently, and who would you be?

Perhaps quiet time with reconciliation,
Revival, renewal of your affiliation.
Why has it taken so long
To get you back to where you belong?

He is looking for those whose love is sincere,
Obedient, and available with a heart of good cheer.
You are living in the end of days;
I encourage you to heed His ways.

His Word—an anchor that is secure,
His incredible love replaces thoughts of fear.
To be here at this time and location,
With disappointments and corruption in our nation.

God has been cast aside.
They attempt to replace Him with arrogance and pride.
No expectations of anyone being kind,
Difficult times ensue; keep that in mind.

Awesome to be His and be in His care,
Knowing His truth we need to share.
For those who asked forgiveness of sin, they choose
The gospel of Christ—good news.

Have a Heart, Preferably a Transplant

My condition was terminal once upon a time.
To give this any thought never entered my mind.
Day by day, year after year, as time passed,
Everything appeared on track; life was moving fast.

One night as I pondered my situation, I lay awake.
Consumed with confusion and sadness, my lip began to quake.
My thoughts startled me, and I found myself shaken.
I questioned my choices—could I have been mistaken?

The world's version of success, I bought the subscription.
It left me empty—a facade, the best description.
I acknowledged something was amiss; so what now?
Deep within, my soul longed for peace, but how?

With no foundation or experience from which to draw,
I called out to the Lord, and to my knees did I fall.
Encompassed by His presence, overwhelmed by a sense of awe,
I willingly surrendered as He responded to my call.

To experience His love, forgiveness, and grace
Left me with a transplanted heart—no scar to trace.
Humbled, as I began to contemplate the cost;
No consideration had been given when I was lost.

This was only the beginning; there was a life plan,
Including commitment and conviction, I began to understand.
Years have passed, each day a gift, a time to serve.
It's been a journey, a never-ending learning curve.

There are many aspects I seek to understand.
I pray to be useful in His ultimate plan.
My desire is strong, and when I feel weak,
I know I'll survive because of the One I seek.

Have you considered your invitation,
Issued by a holy God, requesting your participation?
No surgery required for a transplanted heart;
A desire to surrender to the Holy One is where to start.

He Shared a Precious Gift

With those we love, handle with care;
Our time is limited that we may share.
We each have a calling; we each have a day
When the time has passed for words to say.

Precious memories keep our hearts warm,
Times of sweet remembrance—and at times we are torn.
We've been told time will heal.
There are moments when numbness is all I can feel.

To have loved this much—what a gift!
I close my eyes, see my beloved's smile, and feel my heart lift.
There are times when my soul wants rest.
I press on; for the one I love, I can do nothing less.

Often I think about what my beloved would say or do.
I picture the conversation and know it will see me through.
For me, I choose to praise the Lord.
He shared a precious gift that we both adored.

For my life, He gives me strength.
For me, He has gone to any length
To walk with me, to talk to me,
To reassure me what will someday be.

For now, I will move forward and anticipate.
There will be a day when I will celebrate.
I am calm, knowing in whom I trust.
Eternity with my beloved will be glorious.

Heavenly Father

Heavenly Father, I find the thought difficult
to wrap around my mind.
My association reminds me of my earthly father,
who wasn't there or spent little time.
About holiness, loving Father, and forgiveness, I'm confused.
Accepting that I can trust You, my thoughts are skewed.

Heavenly Father, Your Word states You love me unconditionally,
And Your desire's for me to be bondage free.
I've been chosen and received the call.
However, I struggle with how to surrender all.

Past experiences make it difficult for me to trust,
Yet, deep within me, I know I must.
You've called me forward and made a provision,
Extended grace and patience since my decision.

As I seek You, Lord, through Your Word and prayer,
I'm reminded You love me and I'm in Your care.
I'm grateful for every breath I take,
Reconciling how You gave your life for my sake.

I pray a brother will come alongside,
To mentor me, require accountability, and offer to guide …
Lord, someone who loves You in an incredible way,
Whose life honors You every day.

It's a tall order; I know there are few.
I'll pass it on, I promise You.
Lord, allow me to better understand.
Help me; how do I become a godly man?

Your Word states, "Do Not Fear."
I decided to tape that to my mirror.
Lord, empty me of all my debris.
Let my reflection show more of You and less of me.

Holy Spirit, I sense your nudge.
I forgive my earthly father; I release my grudge.
Heavenly Father, Lord, God, the Holy One,
I am honored to be Your adopted son.

Here I Am

I close my eyes, yet I see.
Lord, may I discern what You speak to me.
I sense Your Spirit; I know You are near.
Lord, open my ears that I may hear.

I'm convinced; I've been persuaded.
Lord, You've stirred my soul and patiently waited.
I caused You grief; I rebuked Your touch.
Lord, You gave your life; You loved me that much.

I acknowledge without You I am helpless;
Lord, apart from the Holy Spirit, I am a mess.
I regret being obstinate and slow to learn,
Lord, I appreciate Your patience, Your great concern.

I contemplate worldly values and morals amiss.
Lord, was I born for a time such as this.
I surrender; I'm available; in You, God, I trust.
Lord, Your righteousness overpowers the unruly, the unjust.

I am weak at my best, yet I will not cower.
Lord, Your covering and protection provide a strong tower.
I have been summoned; I am honored by your request,
Lord, to love You, to give my absolute best.

I love Your Word and the opportunity to share.
Lord, You responded; You answered my prayer.
I hear Your voice; my heart is appeased.
Lord, my mind is content; my soul is pleased.

His Greatest Desire

Did you know I made you special and unique,
And my greatest desire is to be the One you seek?
My provisions, I have bestowed upon you,
And I have been waiting to see you through.

There are very few who will grace My door.
It is not Me they look to ... only a request for more.
More of this, more of that, to take the place of Me,
And I long to open your eyes that you may see.

I am all ... all you will ever need.
When you truly believe this, you will heed.
Take my advice; I give you My Word,
Spend time with me, I promise you will be stirred.

You and Me, one-on-one, pray and fast.
I want a relationship of love—not a task.
Seek those who understand Me in the real sense,
Not as the world teaches with rules and laws so intense.

They miss the mark with all their requests,
And never have an understanding; this is not a test.
It is freedom from what they teach.
My love is all consuming; it is what they should preach.

A condition of the heart,
It is what sets you apart.
It requires a choice, the world or Me?
You decide: what you have now, or to be free.

My life, I did freely give.
For you, forgiveness and opportunity to live.
I want you with Me for eternity.
I am here waiting; what will it be?

Homeland Security

No pat-downs, no metal detector,
No infiltration from any defector.
No security guard, no baggage check,
No X-ray to detect.

No bins for personal items; I learn,
Terrorist threats are of no concern.
No taxes are needed to fund;
It's covered by the Holy One.

No need for border patrol,
Nothing beyond His control.
No trains, planes, or air force;
His plan is right on course.

Arrivals are checked in on time,
No waiting in any line.
Preparations have been made;
The price has been prepaid.

Mercy, grace, and love He extended,
Forgiveness of sins by which, we offended.
Through His Word, I've been told,
Revelations are about to unfold.

A covenant has been provided.
The anticipation should get you excited.
It's personal—a gift presented to me.
Yes, I have Homeland security.

HSD (Holy Spirit Driven)

The diagnosis has been confirmed; I am HSD,
Intensity with purpose and a vision to see.
Random acts of loving kindness will appear;
Calmness in crisis replaces all fear.

One of the symptoms—prayer time—I'm craving,
And a heart condition for those in need of saving.
Absorbing God's Word, exposure is intensified.
My hope: HSD will spread far and wide.

There is no containment; it's all in His hands.
My responsibility's to surrender and submit to His plans.
To sharpen my focus for insight and direction,
I am tested for a by-pass from the world's rejection.

The natural consequences—my heart's aflame.
Overwhelming evidence—I'll never be the same.
With HSD, the effects are not treated;
No supplements or topical cream are needed.

No medication required for best results,
His prescription covers my personal faults.
No treatment necessary with early detection,
I have supplemental coverage with abundant affection.

HSD has consumed my whole being—
A side effect that is completely freeing.
I am His; He is mine.
His transfusion changed my blood line.

I pray for you to have a fervent desire,
To have the same diagnosis transpire.
I am Holy Spirit driven, yes, HSD:
God, Jesus, Holy Spirit—a gift from the Trinity.

I Don't Fit, Thank God

Do you ever feel like you don't fit-
Condescending remarks and you know they want you to quit?
Do you feel like you are going against the grain,
With looks of contempt they can barely contain?

Sometimes subtle, sometimes brash, they criticize.
They may even resort to lies.
Seems like their mission is to hurt;
They put on a smile while being curt.

You have witnessed the abuse of power and the tragedy of greed.
Be encouraged; you have all you need.
As their attitude may seem contrite,
The battle is God's; allow Him the right.

There are principalities at work here—
More at stake than your career.
May I give some advice?
Pray for them in the name of Christ.

God is sovereign and in control.
Allow Him to supervise your role.
He may ask you to stay
And walk you through circumstances day by day.

He may tell you to shake the dust from your feet;
He may have others He wants you to meet.
He may ask you to explain why He died.
Other times, He may ask you to step aside.

He may use you to intercept.
Allow Him to direct your step.
Whatever He desires, follow His lead.
You may be the one to plant a seed.

Your role is to serve, however you can,
And to wait for Him to reveal His plan.
Keep your focus on Him, I suggest.
Through it all, you will be blessed.

I Say Yes, Lord

(Inspired by Patsy Clairmont)

I say yes, Lord, to You this day.
Yes, Lord, to serve You I pray.
Yes, Lord, for Your guidance this day,
Yes, Lord; show me the way.

Yes, Lord, I'll sing Your praise.
Yes, Lord I stand amazed.
Yes, Lord, I'm available to You.
Yes, Lord, it is You I pursue.

Yes, Lord, I surrender my life.
Yes, Lord, I surrender my strife.
Yes, Lord, to the peace You bring.
Yes, Lord, to You, my sovereign King.

Thank You for the breath I take.
Thank You for giving Your life for my sake.
Thank You for loving me, even though …
Thank You for patience as I grow.

Thank You as a new day begins.
Thank You for forgiving my sins.
Thank You for being by my side.
Thank You for arms opened wide.

Thank You, that I might live.
Thank You for a desire to give.
Thank You for a future request.
Thank You for giving me what is best.

No to those who would draw me away.
No to those who have only bad to say.
No to things this world holds dear.
No to unhealthy fear.

No to worldly lust.
No to those I cannot trust.
No to overwhelming drama.
No to those who make up trauma.

No to a day without prayer.
No to those who don't play fair.
No to a day without His lead.
No indeed; I have been freed.

I Stink

Don't get too close; I stink.
And you're the same; that's what I think.
Our righteousness is like filthy rags; we're a stinky mess.
How He could love me is anyone's guess.

We have no reason to be smug or seek entitlements.
There is little we could say that would make any sense.
We need to be cleaned up and edified,
And have someone to trust and walk alongside.

It appears as though we are in the same boat.
Provisions were made for a scapegoat.
You see, someone had to pay; it wasn't free.
A life was given in place of me.

It breaks my heart to know they nailed Him to the cross.
It breaks my heart to know what my sins cost.
There is no debt; it's all been paid.
He gave His life for mine in even trade.

So what do you do with a love like this?
Time for a decision; there is no risk.
Will you come to the same conclusion?
The truth will prevail; there will be no exclusion.

He is Lord; He is God; He is King.
I will rejoice, I will praise, I will sing.
Complete surrender: I am finally free,
And now my reflection shows more of Him and less of me.

If Only

God, thank You for freedom and security.
Through all circumstances, You are there for me.
Your name, everlasting, for a reason,
Our time here temporary—only for a season.

He gives answers in His Word
To know and understand, I'm reassured.
I am not left in disarray;
I can look forward to ultimate peace one day.

Humankind will elevate itself on a pedestal.
Pride and arrogance will be its downfall.
His Word states knowledge will escalate.
Constant self-accreditation seals our fate.

Earthquakes, famines, droughts: there will be more.
Hurricanes and tornadoes, the count higher than before …
The time has come to make a choice:
To seek God's truth, forgiveness—to rejoice.

Or to continue on in a state of denial.
Tribulation is coming; there will be a trial.
If only you would seek Him and make a request—
If only you would trust, He could give you rest.

If only you would surrender to the Holy One—
Jesus Christ, the Savior, God's Son.
Feeling confused, perhaps it's a condition of the heart.
Maybe it's time for a jump-start.

No decision is a decision in itself.
No one is buried with power or wealth.
To surrender to Christ and ask Him to forgive
Will be the very first time you begin to live.

It Is What I Pray

Heavenly Father, whom I adore,
What do you ask, what is in store?
May I have opportunity to serve You today.
I seek your direction; it is what I pray.

O Lord, let me be wise,
With gifts and talents You will utilize,
For Your purpose is what I aspire.
Of Your plans may I never tire.

Let me be the one who serves
With boldness and steel nerves.
For You, Lord, may I go to any length.
For Your glory, I pray for strength.

May I surrender all of me.
May I be found to be worthy.
O Lord, help me to understand
Where I fit best into Your plan.

Give me a listening ear
To clearly hear
How I may serve You today.
O Lord, it is what I pray.

Keep the Change

For most of us change does not come naturally.
We become comfortable—routines are set—I
think most of you would agree.
Situations arise and priorities may need to be rearranged.
At the time it may not make sense, may be even a bit strange.

God's voice is sometimes loud and clear.
There are other times when I question what I hear.
When there is open communication and you seek to understand,
You realize an invitation has been extended
to be a part of His plan.

When He has given notification,
You will want to follow through with anticipation.
How important to have a listening ear.
One of God's most stated commands: do not fear.

If you will follow through with His request,
You'll have opportunity to see Him bless.
Keep in mind His plans are perfect and true.
Allow the Holy Spirit to motivate you.

As we step out of our comfort zone,
Change is not easy; sometimes we moan and groan.
Looking back into our past, change is good.
Perhaps as we reflect, it is better understood.

Change is required to move us in His direction.
He has our best interest, perhaps a course correction.
Our schedules may require a transformation.
Sometimes life appears to be a continuous alteration.

When you receive a nudge from the Holy Spirit, action is required.
Don't let what-ifs keep you from being inspired.
Life here is fleeting, temporary, and will not last.
Keep the change, and then let it pass.

Let the Past Be Past

My life compares to a reality series:
Cause and effect, there seems a multitude of theories.
Some may describe me as a hot mess—
An accurate description, I must confess.

My path has left me bruised and battered,
To the point my value no longer mattered.
A less cluttered life is what I seek.
I am determined not to be faint or weak.

I am seeking counsel and tools to cope.
I am seeking renewal and opportunity for hope.
How often we attempt to survive on our own,
Only to realize we don't need to walk alone.

Running away from past behavior
Led me front and center to Christ the Savior.
I knock at the door and seek the holy King,
Choosing to experience the peace He will bring.

His desire to forgive me and let the past be past,
The relief He provides—difficult for my mind to grasp.
Words cannot describe as I surrendered my will—
The void in my heart, His Holy Spirit did fill.

A renewal of my mind, a change of heart,
An opportunity provided for a new start.
My prayer, O Lord, my desire I would say:
May I have a personal encounter with you today …

Me, Me, Me

Need help, what's in it for me?
Before I commit, what's it to be?
Always looking out for number one,
I'm all about making sure I have fun.

Those I foresee in my path
Will likely experience some of my wrath.
Me-itus—how could it be a disease,
When I'm the only one to please?

Me, Me, Me:
I love all three.
I'm always at the top of my list—
No exception, I won't take the risk.

Thoughts of me come so quick,
How could this be considered sick?
It's part of my MO.
It's been about me so long it's all I know.

Where will this eventually lead?
Out of control, much like a weed?
Is it possible there is an antibiotic?
All about me feels quite narcotic.

When it's not about me, I go into a tailspin.
Some have suggested my behavior is sin.
Now that's a word you don't hear anymore.
It strikes right at the core.

Just the thought brings on fear.
Why, I might even shed a tear.
I don't even want to go there.
Changing my behavior seems unfair.

My love for me has become emphatic.
I know you will think it to be dramatic.
Selfish and inconsiderate have become the rage.
I'm always the first to engage.

If I were to look beyond myself,
It may be overwhelming to my health.
I'd probably have the shakes and withdrawals
If I were to look at my character flaws.

How do I get over me?
Is there a chance I could break free?
I'm told it's possible if I surrender to Him.
Sincerity's at the root; it can't be a whim.

They say He will give me opportunity
To be totally free of me.
Introduce me to the Son,
Jesus—He is the One.

As He removed my disguise
And opened my eyes,
Revealing the lies I've told myself in the past,
He set me free at last.

What's in it for me?
Now I see ...
A new beginning where I am free
To love the Lord, and you more than me.

Restoration is what He does best.
His incredible love heals me, nothing less.
What's in it for me?
I know where I'll spend eternity.

Mediocre at Best

I've followed my own path, set my own course.
My disregard of knowing Him has left me with remorse.
The world's pull seems to entice me away,
A description of my faith—lukewarm, I would say.

His Word, I seek occasionally when I feel the draw.
I spend more time worshipping the greatest, latest offer at the mall.
Many options are available in which to medicate,
And consequences elude me to consider or contemplate.

One foot in the world, while claiming a faith,
I am the one His Word describes as chafe.
I know what I know and to myself I lie.
The truth will prevail before and after I die.

Slowly and surely my world begins to unravel.
The path I have chosen, I don't recommend you travel.
At times my faith has been mediocre at best.
On my own, I've yet to experience peace or rest.

Lightly salted would describe where I'm at.
It's only the beginning; I pray to move forward from that.
As time begins to unwind,
I pray to God that I will not be left behind.

Mediocre with God reveals I don't trust or really believe.
To acknowledge this fact causes my heart to grieve.
His Word states we will reap what we've sown.
My desire, to become one of God's very own.

Today, I make a declaration:
My heart, I surrender for restoration.
Mediocre at best, lukewarm, describes my life no more.
To love Christ, to live in Christ, is what I was designed for.

Now Is the Time

Now is the time; stake your claim
To belong to Him—never be the same.
Complete surrender makes burdens light.
His way is always to set things right.

We were never designed to be on our own.
This is temporary; we are here on loan.
Inquire of Him to reveal His plan;
Be prepared to take His hand.

He will make provision for whatever He has asked.
You will be equipped to complete the task.
What a privilege to be in His will.
The peace makes my heart go still.

Life is messy and requires grace,
Looking forward to the day we are face-to-face.
Our time is getting close, you see.
Give Him your heart; that is the key.

For here and now we run the race.
Now is the time to pick up the pace.
No need to wait and see.
His desire for you is to be free.

Now is the time to submit to prayer.
He will lead you to those who need His care.
Choose the Lord; He is more than a friend.
He paid the price; He died for our sin.

The finish line is getting near.
Now is the time—no need to fear.
May we give all honor and praise,
To reside with You, Lord, all of our days.

Now is the time, you can finally rest.
As a member of God's family; you are blessed.
Life is but a glimpse, you see.
We yearn to see You for eternity.

Oh, Brother

Who has the strength to make a stand?
Who will place themselves in God's hand?
Are you willing to call out the behavior?
Are you willing to represent the Savior?

Here I am, Lord, voicing your concern.
I pray for wisdom and a heart to discern.
There's no pleasure calling out someone who is a façade.
I surrender in obedience to follow through, as directed by God.

There are those who treat God's Word amiss.
Have you been exposed to someone like this?
Abusive power and arrogance are the roots of the sin.
The collateral damages occur once and again.

Continuing to boast with elevated esteem,
Entitlements with a personal theme.
This will end in a sad state—
The totality difficult to estimate.

Coveting a personal agenda, God's Word is skewed,
While displaying a smug attitude.
Disagreeing with you, your vision, your intent,
You rearrange God's Word and ask others to repent.

Oh, brother, your iniquity has become a snare,
I have concern for those you have treated unfair.
Are you willing to look at issues to address?
Will you continue to digress?

Oh, brother, I hear you speaking *Christianese*.
There are symptoms indicating a heart disease.
One day the Lord will judge,
The sin, the nature, and those who begrudge.

My heart is filled with sadness and sorrow.
The time is now, today; don't wait for tomorrow.
Oh, brother, will you call upon God
To clear your slate and expose your fraud?

A holy God understands you are off course.
His voice is calling; consider the source.
Your opportunity is now; your decision is what it's about.
Will you respond to God or resent me for calling you out?

Peace, Be Still

Oh, for a quiet moment or two,
I close my eyes, and envision You.
It is a calm I have never known.
I am certain, I am not alone.

Your presence fills my mind—
An experience that slows time.
In that moment there are no fears,
I sense Your Spirit; I am moved to tears.

I am perfectly calm.
I feel no qualms.
I ask myself, How can this be?
How could You have such love for me?

As I try to understand,
You reach out to take my hand …
As You lead me down the path,
My joy overwhelms; I begin to laugh.

Could this be a dream?
For a moment it would seem …
And then I hear a whispered voice;
My heart leaps and I rejoice.

My Lord desires for me to be free,
Spending time with Him is up to me.
As I surrender my will,
He whispers, "Peace, be still."

Please, Be Seeded

An answer to prayer, I am anticipating.
Each and every seat has been waiting
For someone in need of salvation—
Someone who desires to understand creation.

For someone looking to know the Word,
Someone wanting the heart to be stirred ...
A time to connect,
A time to reflect.

Someone with a hurting heart,
Someone needing a new start,
Someone seasoned with faith that's strong,
Someone who longs to praise through song.

Those who want solid Bible teaching,
An appreciation for awesome preaching,
Will you join me and pray for each empty seat?
Will you extend an invitation to those you meet?

Friends, family, and neighbors—pray for them.
May their hearts be softened toward Him.
Will you be the one to plant some seeds—
Allow the Master gardener to control the weeds?

Do you have a future in broadcasting?
Will you respond to the everlasting?
One empty chair, you are needed,
For standing room only; please, be seeded.

Power Up

Power: an inherent ability many desire.
Power: an authority so many want to acquire …
A determination to rule and have dominion,
To escalate the value of their own opinions.

All this hype regarding authority and influence,
Temptations abound; situations are tense.
For some, it allows them to have their own way,
With no respect for what God's Word has to say.

They sincerely believe they control their own destiny.
With a mind-set firm, they have little regard for you or me.
To question their motives causes them to scoff.
Whatever they determine, their theology is off.

God's Word is available to all men.
No consideration, no compliance, repeat history again.
Trying to justify yourselves before men,
God knows your heart and your sin.

God is all powerful; when you know this is true,
Circuits are connected from Him to you.
Will you belong to the King of Kings, the Holy One?
Will you desire a relationship with Christ, God's Son?

His concern's for you to be covered and protected,
Since before the time He was resurrected.
He offers you a saving grace.
He will take your sin and leave no trace.

The power of man is a passing phase.
A limit has been set for the end of days.
Living out life is revelation.
It allows you freedom and celebration.

Today, ask Him to forgive your sin,
Time is of the essence to get plugged in.
He will provide a strong tower.
Will you be the one to experience God's power?

Pretender or Contender?

If today, you were called into court,
Would there be enough evidence to support
The Christian you claim to be?
Or would they decide to set you free?

If witnesses were called in,
Would you have a chance to win?
If probing questions were asked,
How long do you think you could last?

If you were asked about time in prayer,
Would this bring on an empty stare?
Your relationship with Jesus, would you profess?
Or is this a question you would prefer not to address?

If you were asked to take the stand,
Could you explain God's providential plan?
When asked about the Holy Spirit, what would you say?
Would you be direct or give an answer that's gray?

If we were to audit your checking account,
Would you be embarrassed with your donation amount?
If you were asked if your faith was firm,
Would this cause you to squirm?

Would there be conviction in your defense,
Or would your answers be on the fence?
Would they grant you a continuance to refile,
Or would they consider you to be hostile?

One day you will be face-to-face.
The King of Kings will judge your case.
No court, no questions, no jury,
It will be past time to worry.

You should make a decision today.
He is the only way.
This could be your last opportunity.
May your eyes be open to see.

He died to take your place—
An incredible display of grace.
He is all you will ever need.
How will you proceed?

Really, Who Made the Rules Anyway?

Are rules made for those who want their own way?
Are they for those who don't know how to play?
Are they made to keep you in line?
Or are they made to put on a sign?

There are rules for this and rules for that,
For some to be called on the mat.
Are rules made for motley fools?
Or are they made to give us tools?

Rules for those who love to please,
Rules provide comfort for type A personalities.
Rules for those who like to disagree,
There are rules that don't suit me.

Rules to give a sense of order,
Rules about who can cross the border.
Rules as to when you can arrive,
And rules to know before you drive.

Rules about how to behave,
Rules about how to save.
There are rules of the road,
Rules when you haul a load.

Rules for your household,
Rules that you've been told,
Rules on the job,
Rules to handle a surly mob.

Rules to pay your tax,
Rules that come through on a fax,
There are rules in any sport,
There are rules of every sort.

Rules to follow at your work,
Rules that make you want to smirk,
There are rules that you appreciate
Rules about being late.

There are rules about being fair,
Rules about how to share,
There are rules about tradition,
Rules about nutrition.

And what about schools?
They always have their rules.
What about government?
Are there rules how your money is spent?

Rules ... are they for our best?
Or are they mostly some sort of test?
Rules seem to set the mode,
Rules—there seems to be an overload.

Really, who made the rules anyway?
The answer, I would say,
I'm more interested in the *ruler of all*,
I'm interested in responding to His call.

I want to reflect His glory.
I want that to be my story.
I want to be on my knees.
It is Him I want to please.

Couldn't we just do what is right,
Knowing He has us in His sight?
In His Word, the rules, there are only ten—
Commandments for women, children, and men.

He gave Ten Commands we should heed.
They would suffice for all we need.
I recommend you read His book.
Give it a closer look.

Ask Him to speak through His Word.
May your understanding be reassured.
If you were to meet with Him today,
Would you be okay?

Redeemer Rewards Card

At the end of time, will you have points to redeem?
Or will you awaken from what appears to be a dream?
Will your rewards card include a heavenly bonus?
Or will you see earthly treasure consumed by rust?

Will your service to God yield a vast storehouse of rewards?
If left on your own, how will your points be scored?
Will the righteous Lord offer you a crown?
Or, are you on the highway of life, looking for a turn-around?

Each of us will have rewards according to our labor.
Will you have points voided—yourself out of favor?
Were you seeking to please others, with points exempt?
On all accounts, will you be held in contempt?

Will you be the one who lays up treasure?
Or will you be found without merit or measure?
Will you recognize He gave His life for your sake?
Will you receive the point? What will it take?

Christ will credit your every act, word, and thought.
Will you be left reconciling what His Word taught?
His rewards card has no expiration date,
Issued by the One who is exceedingly great.

There are no hidden fees.
Benefits are sure to please.
Once issued, cancellation period—never.
A binding agreement: eternity ... forever.

Will you make application?
Begin the process of sanctification?
Apply in person; let the points accrue.
Today, the offer is available to you.

Salt and Light

Destructive behaviors and willful abuse,
A degrading society with morals loose …
Hurting and hopeless—an adverse situation,
With numbers expanding throughout the nation.

Corruption, entitlement issues, and senseless greed,
An endless list of those in need.
There are those many would want to label,
Describing their condition as volatile and unstable.

Worldly values and dysfunctional relationships,
For such a time as this, our God equips.
Rely on the Lord; He will make a provision.
Prepare for battle; His Word creates great division.

Today may be the last of your chances.
Are you understanding the current circumstances?
We've been called to be salt and light,
To make a stand for what is right.

The time is coming; it is very near.
Your commitment to Christ will cause some to jeer.
A limitation has been set for the end of days—
A blessing for those who walk in His ways.

It is up to you and to me to share His hope,
To be there for those who can barely cope.
In your circle of influence will you be found?
Will you respond to His call as opportunities abound?

Are you a reflection of Christ?
Are you willing to make a sacrifice?
Do you have the spiritual insight?
You have been chosen; will you be salt and light?

Stirred and Shaken, Not Forsaken

Memories are stirred; I ask myself, remember when?
I reminisce over things I would like to do over again.
I did the best I could in my unsaved condition—
Worldly views that did not comply with tradition.

I remember a groaning in my spirit and seeking to understand.
He explained my condition and His ultimate plan.
I was weak and visibly shaken
As He touched my heart and promised I would not be forsaken.

If I could have the wisdom and knowledge of today,
To start over and ask Him to have His way,
From the beginning, I would seek His face,
As His Word permeates, I would appreciate His grace.

When I focus on Him, rather than circumstances,
Perseverance and endurance are not left to chances.
His Spirit edifies me with peace and calm.
I am reminded how much He loves me in the 139th psalm.

Now I have opportunity to serve, as directed,
My Lord and God, the One who was resurrected,
To make myself available, to be obedient to His voice.
Each day, I am assured He has given me a choice.

As long as I have breath, may I choose to serve
In response to a holy love I do not deserve.
In conclusion, the past cannot be changed.
Let me move forward with priorities rearranged.

Let me awaken each morning with a resounding yes
For His purpose, His plans, His requests.
My hope, my trust in Jesus, the Holy One—
My greatest desire: to hear Him say, "Job well done."

When we meet face-to-face
At a predetermined time, in a heavenly place,
I await with anticipation
My final destination.

Test-a-Money

Sixty-six books inspired by the Lord,
His holy Word a two-edged sword ...
A love letter on a scale that is grand,
Designed for us, an individual benefit plan.

Malachi 3:10 states, "Put Him to the test."
It is His Word; we are not to treat it in jest.
Not a suggestion, a written command,
To fill up the storehouse; it is part of His plan.

We say we love Him and ask for His favor.
He asked us to give, and it prompts us to waiver.
When the subject is raised regarding tithes,
Blood pressure rises; we break out in hives.

We ask the Lord, may our needs be met.
When He reminds us to give, we begin to fret.
We solicit the Lord in an emergency situation.
We look for Him to be our filling station.

About money, think how often we fuss.
The bottom line: our tithe equals our trust.
May I give a suggestion?
His Word, why should we question?

He is faithful and wants to bless.
Lack of obedience causes our own distress.
Ask Him to change the condition of our heart;
Be prepared for the blessings to start.

Tell me again about the One we love and trust.
Is our offering acceptable or unjust?
Are we for real or somewhat phony?
Giving should be a part of our testimony.

We will never be able to out give Him.
His abundant love will flow over the brim.
He is waiting to give us His best.
His challenge to us: put Him to the test.

That's Life

Life is full of challenges and circumstances,
Opportunities, if needed, for second chances.
I am a work in progress on a journey—
A never-ending learning experience, you may agree.

God's Word, as I make an effort to meditate,
My heart begins to resonate.
I have more trust and less concern
As I await with anticipation His return.

My adoption papers have already been filed.
I have the reality of living life as His child.
My spirit is kindred, light as a feather.
I'm connected to my heavenly Father, Lord, and King forever.

Trials and tribulations can easily make us weary.
Adversity appears with days dark and dreary.
This is temporary; keep it in mind.
The real treasure in life—a precious find.

In His Word, God has a purpose and plan,
A guiding light for those who understand.
He overshadows the latest in personal security
With step-by-step instructions to be bondage-free.

Should you begin your day with time in prayer,
Ask Him to direct your path in His care.
Absorb His Word with expectation.
Surrender to Him with anticipation.

Choices will be made every day.
Will you be on your own or ask Him to have His way?
What about you?
Who or what will you pursue?

The time is coming; it is very near.
Many will experience anxiety and fear.
A solid rock, a foundation, to know Him I must.
Today, where will you place your trust?

The AudaCity

Do you live in AudaCity, population of one?
Are you there alone because everyone else is done?
With a history of remarks that hurt and sometimes harm,
You exhibit no hint of any kind of charm.

Should you decide you want to get over you,
Look in the mirror and say, "Me, myself, and I are through."
At first you may be a little scared.
Change takes some time; be prepared.

A trip down memory lane with old tapes
May have you looking for a fire escape.
Dredging through those past files
Will likely create some new trials.

Reasoning with the past, you may need to address.
It's an intricate part of the healing process.
Sorting out the whys and whats
May reveal how you became such a putz.

As God is in the restoration business,
He offers opportunity to survive your mess.
The process begins with surrender; it's the only way.
There is work to be done; you'll want to start today.

Repentance and sorrow will follow if you are sincere.
You may need to apologize to those who are near.
God is sufficient and knows your need.
He is waiting for you to allow Him to lead.

I hope, indeed, you are stirred and shaken.
Through renewal you will not be forsaken.
By outward appearance, we are all perishing.
The light of Christ's Gospel is what we should be cherishing.

The end is near; have you prepared?
Don't be left behind with those who are scared.
You have a responsibility:
Are you who God has called you to be?

The Eleventh Hour

There are times when, in our mind,
We have a sense God is hard to find.
Why is it we think that way?
Why do we struggle, feeling that is okay?

He is all knowing and has eyes on us,
So why are we temperamental and put up a fuss?
Why are we trying to put Him to the test,
When it is usually a result of our mess?

Other times it is due to circumstance,
Or the same old song we present—the same old dance.
Our attempts to make Him fit in our mold,
If not to our liking, our hearts turn cold.

When we are looking to have our wish list met,
And want instant results with no regrets,
At the eleventh hour, pushing eleven fifty-five,
Sometimes it seems we may not survive.

God's intervention appears slow to us.
Perhaps it is to teach us to trust.
And how much faith comes into play?
If you were to answer, what would you say?

God knows exactly what we need.
It works best when we allow Him to lead.
Should we take a good look at ourselves?
Consider our conditions? Take His Word from the shelf?

You are the one He continues to pursue.
Will you receive His love for you?
Only then will you understand His power.
Why wait until the eleventh hour?

The End Result

(Inspired by Charles Stanley)

For your faith, suffering you will face.
With God's help, you can respond with grace.
Your path will be paved with persecution.
Will you become bitter or grow as part of the solution?

God knows what you will endure.
Your future, He knows what will occur.
Life can be painful and difficult.
You should remain hopeful for the end result.

In your position, what are the chances,
You will be exposed to dire circumstances?
The situation is temporary; keep it in mind.
Focus on the Lord as things begin to unwind.

It will happen if you are a genuine believer.
Multitudes parade in line with the deceiver.
Don't be disappointed or filled with dismay.
Keep in mind what the Lord has to say.

He will never leave you nor forsake you.
He has revealed Himself and you know what is true.
The story has been written and you know the end.
He gave His life for you, my friend.

Prepare yourself; you may have trouble for a time.
Circumstances can change like the turn of a dime.
Take this opportunity to bless the holy
King who walks us through fires
With an attitude of gratitude, no matter what transpires.

Into His Word I need to delve a little deeper.
I want to honor my promise keeper.
Through Christ, I can do awe things,
May I be found honorable to the King of Kings.

The Grand Stand

There will be a day
When you will stand up and say,
What about freedom? What about rights?
Why was I passive? That is my plight.

Shouldn't I have taken a stand?
Is it past time to draw a line in the sand?
There comes a time when you realize
You have been told so many lies.

Lies of those who care for you, or so they claim,
Difficult to distinguish; they all appear to be the same.
It may wise to investigate.
You could discover it may not be too late.

You may be disappointed with what you find.
You can make a difference if you will take the time.
Take on the responsibility;
Freedom has never been free.

Are you prepared? Do you understand
The freedoms you are losing in this land?
A few in power, consumed with greed—
Pretenders without intentions to meet your need.

You have a privilege not granted to all,
A responsibility to respond to the call.
Take time to pray; vote your conviction in the selection.
You may be the one who decides the election.

Neither may qualify for the moral majority.
However, a choice is necessary for you and me.
Today, make a decision for the situations at hand.
Are you willing to make a grand stand?

The Mirror

I look in the mirror; I look in my eyes.
Will someone see beyond my disguise?
I have a picture; I let people see,
And then there is the real me.

So many times I pick myself apart.
I tell myself I don't measure up; I'm not that smart.
When I'm alone, I'm left with what I see.
The reflection in the mirror doesn't please me.

Contemplating a holy God seems beyond consideration.
I add that to my pile of frustration.
Sometimes I imagine what it would be like to be free.
I question if He would want to do that for me.

My soul longs for truth and honesty.
Will I ever be comfortable with me?
What am I really giving up—my disguise,
My self-talk, frivolous concerns, hurtful lies?

If I were to reprioritize my day,
Start with His Word, prayer, and ask Him to have His way,
If change is required, what will it take?
A transformation—a total remake.

A commitment from me will begin the process.
My self-talk causes me to regress.
I think about who I am now, and remember where I came from.
I pray for wisdom that I might overcome.

Upon my surrender, a great release ensued.
The lightness I felt changed my attitude.
He offers me unconditional love and peace for sure,
And a promise to see me through circumstances I may endure.

I pray for my life to reflect His glory.
I pray for others; this could be their story.
Now when I look in the mirror, I like what I see:
A reflection of who the Lord made me to be.

The Ultimate Offer

Today, I recall the time when I asked myself, is this all there is?
I had limited knowledge and no experience
of what it meant to be His.
All my needs were met; yet I was aware of a void, a gap.
I had feelings of inadequacy; life appeared to be a trap.

I wasn't sure where to begin or how to pray.
Spontaneous reaction brought me to my knees that day.
I remember feelings of sorrow and humiliation,
Asking for forgiveness and opportunity for transformation.

I began to understand this is a life process.
There will always be issues to address.
He asked me to move on, not linger in the past.
From a worldly view to belief and faith—what a contrast!

His Word served as an anchor, a lifeline.
I became a work in process through renewing of my mind.
My highest priority: to love Him intimately,
To surrender to His plans to work in and through me.

As I remember back to that day,
For those who find themselves in a similar
situation, I'm reminded to pray.
God's Word breathes life for those who choose.
May I explain what you have to lose?

To make no commitment or have no concern,
There may be no other opportunity given for you to discern
A holy God who offers a gift from the Savior:
Eternal life not based on your past behavior.

You have received the ultimate offer.
Will you respond to His love or remain a scoffer?
Heaven or hell—you decide
Where in eternity will you reside …

Understanding the good news He has shared,
I pray you are now prepared.
Ask Him to forgive your sin.
Today, let your life in Christ begin.

The Voice

The voice—not a TV series or vocal competition.
No blind auditions, knock-out rounds, or votes for attrition.
No way to chart, no way to measure,
His voice is life-changing, more valuable than earthly treasure.

When your mind and heart are meshed together,
And the Holy Spirit lifts you like a feather,
You quiet your spirit and seek His voice.
You understand the blessing; you understand the choice.

His voice, His presence, I know for sure—
Sometimes soft and gentle, barely a whisper ...
Sometimes loud and resounding, I hear Him speak,
Humbled, blessed, and privileged, I feel meek.

I hear the voice; I receive the connection—
Sometimes encouragement, sometimes correction.
The choice is mine to lean in or pull away—
A decision for me to make today.

Listening with my head and heart,
I realize I have been set apart.
His instructions differ from you to me,
Each of us a tapestry designed purposefully.

Will you extend an invitation, you who have ears?
He has been waiting patiently, perhaps years ...
A sovereign, holy God awaits with anticipation,
The one who has known you since before creation.

The way has been prepared.
The truth has been shared.
Now it is up to you to make a choice.
Blessed are those who seek His voice.

The Warehouse

Bring your imagination with me.
It's the warehouse I want you to see:
Beautiful gifts boxed with bows—
So many; the number, no one knows.

Let's open one and look inside.
I'm a little curious, I must confide.
It takes my breath away.
I am speechless; words I cannot say.

Let's open a second gift.
This one is large, the lid difficult to lift.
It seems to be filled to the brim,
Wrapped eloquently with lovely trim.

One more, let's take a peek.
I look inside; I feel weak …
Beautiful gifts, too many to count.
There seems to be an exorbitant amount.

I tell myself, *I don't understand,*
And then I glimpse a copy of the Master's plan.
All the gifts, He would provide.
All the gifts, He set aside.

And then to me it did occur,
I should ask to be sure.
Were the gifts available to be shared?
Yes, for those He loved and for whom he cared.

Gifts unopened because there was no request,
Gifts unopened because they settled for something less ...
Gifts unopened because they didn't believe,
Gifts they didn't ask to receive.

As soon as I could become stable,
I gathered the list and considered the label.
How many boxes of love were left behind?
How many boxes of faith—a number I couldn't find.

How many boxes of prophecy,
How many boxes of peace, I couldn't see?
How many boxes of servanthood?
There were so many from where I stood.

The warehouse was monumental in size;
To continue the search did not seem wise.
I stopped to pray and seek direction
And was pointed to a particular section.

There were boxes of invitations.
The Holy Spirit existed at this location.
It appeared very surreal,
An embossed verse written on each seal.

The gift of the Holy Spirit, He grants.
This is a spiritual implant.
He is all consuming.
There will be no assuming.

If you have this gift, it will show—
A gift for those who believe and know.
He has made a provision
For when you make your decision.

All the gifts stored online,
Every one marked divine.
Some on the shelf had dust;
Others were stamped In God We Trust.

As all the gifts are offered free,
There is no need for a return policy.
Do you foresee a possible solution?
Will you be a recipient in the distribution?

The warehouse was created
Not to be complicated.
Close your eyes with me and pray.
Do you see the warehouse empty one day?

It is His desire,
You would choose to aspire.
Before you leave, for those who believe,
Ask, and you shall receive.

Today

(Inspired by His grace)

I find myself in an anxious state.
My soul is stirred; I can no longer wait.
I have a surreal awareness of heaven and hell.
Emotions overwhelm me; my heart begins to swell.

I am a sinner; that is where I will begin.
My life has been lived with unrepentant sin.
On my own, I am stuck in my old behavior.
God, I seek Your forgiveness; I am in need of a savior.

I believe your Son, Jesus Christ shed His blood on the cross for me.
I believe your Word; He died that I may be free.
I surrender my life and pray for transformation.
I confess Jesus Christ as my Lord and accept His offer of salvation.

I believe Jesus was on the cross and for my sins, He bled,
And on the third day God raised Christ from the dead.
I am before you today—an extension of Your grace.
No longer will I walk alone through situations I face.

I have peace, joy in my heart—
An opportunity given for a new start.
I accept Your gift, eternal life; I no longer fear the grave.
My name is written in Your book; today I am saved.

Distractions will present themselves each day—
Guidelines available in His Word and opportunities to pray.
This is when you begin to live, to rejoice.
When a decision is made, it is your choice.

My prayer for you to understand:
God has purposed the ultimate plan.
Our time is limited; perhaps today,
Will you accept His offer? What do you say?

Until Death Do Us Part

(Inspired by a skeptic)

My favorite quotation: "If it is to be, it's up to me."
I believe I control my own destiny.
As I check my reflection, I'm okay with what I see.
Comparing myself to others, I'm more than comfortable with me.

Occasionally, I experience a speed bump in life.
I search myself for options to handle the strife.
I've done quite well on my own, I would say.
I've stood my ground and survived this way.

I'm completely happy with life thus far.
For my goals and dreams, I'm right on par.
As I pondered the world's version of success,
Priorities were compromised, some values put to the test.

Believer, a word to describe a few I know personally,
Their convictions appear as foreign territory to me.
Okay for them—for me, not so much,
I've always considered them to be some kind of crutch.

And then it happened; believers disappeared in the light.
The media tried to explain it away, linked to a terrorist sight.
Given all considerations, when the verdict came in,
The evidence to me appeared weak and thin.

In the twinkling of an eye,
They disappeared into the sky.
I was numb, now uncertain of my belief,
And no matter how I evaluated it, there was no relief.

Those who believed in Christ, they were no more.
Unsettled would describe me; I was shaken to the core.
I don't know the time or date.
I am assured my lack of faith sealed my fate.

As I began to awaken from what appeared to be a dream,
Reality set in and it was true, or so it seemed.
"Until death do us part," the words haunted me.
Today, was I given a glimpse of the future to be?

Unwrapped

(Inspired by Pastor Andrew Murch's sermon)

One may define a wrap:
To wind, to fold, a covering that may overlap.
Another description: to envelop, to surround—
An outer garment enclosed all around.

We can be wrapped up, absorbed,
Devoted, engrossed with implications scored ...
To wrap up, to make final, to conclude,
To summarize statements and reports accrued.

To unwrap, to be opened, to undo, to reveal,
Vulnerability; how uncomfortable it makes us feel.
There can be many layers to unwrap—
Hidden compartments that feel like a trap.

Harboring secrets, tarnished with regret,
Living with lies you would like to forget ...
Painful decisions that you chose,
Now a cover story stands exposed.

Uncertain if all can be forgiven,
Feelings develop that are fear driven.
There is relief available if you so desire,
Incredible love, and all you require.

Unwrapped, exposed, somewhat bare,
Covered by His blood, given to His care ...
For you, He has a plan, a specific purpose:
Inclusive restoration, forgiveness, and trust.

Unwrapped, surrendered sorrow and grief,
An offer extended for permanent relief ...
Unwrapped, you have nothing to prove,
However, a decision is required for your next move.

Unwrapped is the present, the gift eternal,
An invitation to create a new journal.
Unwrapped and uncovered from piles of debris,
Through His love, He gave His life for you and me.

What Is Truth?

What is truth? A question for you today.
If you were to respond, what would you say?
One may say it is relative to the situation at hand.
Others suggest, it is difficult to understand.

Many say circumstances dictate what may imply,
The importance for others; truth does not apply.
Some claim it is an area that is gray,
And there are those who think it can change day to day.

Where do you stand on the battlefield?
Have you asked for truth to be revealed?
Nothing but the truth, so help me God—a familiar phrase.
To better understand, we can look at God's ways.

Truth, a solid foundation, a non-wavering baseline,
Reality, correctness, accuracy are words that define.
Jesus is the way, the truth, the life; it is His Word.
Understanding who He is, you may be assured.

To walk in truth, to believe the Word of God, and to obey,
The power of the Spirit will guide you along the way.
To know truth may help you escape snares,
And protect you from those who put on airs.

The Spirit of the truth is stated in His Word.
For scoffers with scales this is absurd.
Today, arrogance and pride set the tone.
It will not end well for those on their own.

If it is truth you seek, you have opportunity today.
He is waiting; take time to pray.
Ask Him to forgive and clear the slate.
Ask Him to open your eyes and change your fate.

For those who believe, you have been sealed.
His truth shall be your armored shield.
He gave His life for me and you; I know for sure.
His Word is truth; He will forever endure.

CPSIA information can be obtained at www.ICGtesting.com
Printed in the USA
LVOW08s1311310316

481599LV00001B/32/P